creative crafts from
plastic
bottles

By Nikki Connor
Illustrated by Sarah-Jane Neaves

Copper Beech Books
Brookfield, Connecticut

© Aladdin Books Ltd 1997
Designed and produced by
Aladdin Books Ltd
28 Percy Street
London W1P 0LD

First published in the United States
in 1997 by
Copper Beech Books,
an imprint of
The Millbrook Press
2 Old New Milford Road
Brookfield, Connecticut 06804

Design David West Children's Book
Design
Illustrator Sarah-Jane Neaves
Photographer Roger Vlitos

Library of Congress Cataloging-in-
Publication Data

Connor, Nikki. Plastic bottles / by Nikki
Connor ; illustrated by Sarah-Jane Neaves.
p. cm. -- (Creative crafts from)
Summary: Provides
instructions for making such items as
bracelets, a rocket, a buggy, and a plant
pot from plastic bottles.
ISBN 0-7613-0553-X (lib. bdg.). --
1. Toy making--Juvenile literature.
2. Plastic bottles--Juvenile literature.
3. Plastic scrap--Juvenile literature
[1. Plastic craft. 2. Handicraft.] I. Neaves,
Sarah-Jane, ill. II. Title. III. Series: Connor,
Nikki. Creative crafts from--.
TT174.C66   1997   96-45580
745.57'2--dc21   CIP AC

Contents

Before you start
skittles
flowerpot
maracas
bracelets
mobile
submarine
windmill
catamaran
space shuttle
racing car
color chart

Before you start

A "what you need" ingredients panel appears with the photograph of each project. Decide which project you are going to make and collect everything you need.

The red, yellow, and blue paint cups mean that you need poster paints. All colors (except white) can be made by mixing together a combination of these three. See the color chart at the back of this book to find out how. You may choose instead to use ready mixed colors if you have them.

Use a pencil point to punch holes in paper or thin plastic. For thicker cardboard and plastic, you may need to use scissors - <u>ask an adult to help</u>.

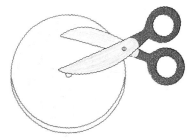

A dotted line in the instructions means you are to fold, not cut. A solid line shows where to cut.

Only use scissors that are especially designed for children's crafts. They usually have rounded ends. Always have an adult with you when you use them.

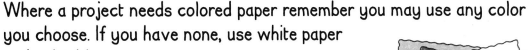

Where a project needs colored paper remember you may use any color you choose. If you have none, use white paper and paint it!

If you follow the step-by-step instructions carefully you will be sure to finish up with a successful model - but if you prefer to use these designs just as ideas to get you started, then that's fine too!

Have fun.

skittles

plastic bottles

paintbrush

poster paints

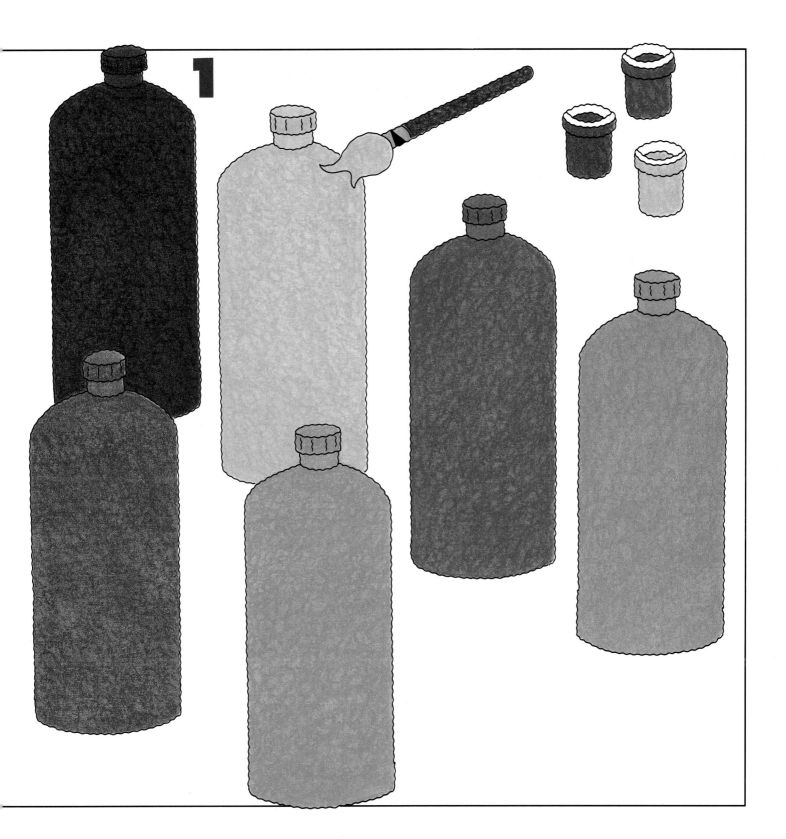

flowerpot

plastic bottle

scissors

paintbrush

poster paints

1

2

maracas

plastic bottles

wooden dowels

paintbrush

rice grains

adhesive tape

poster paints

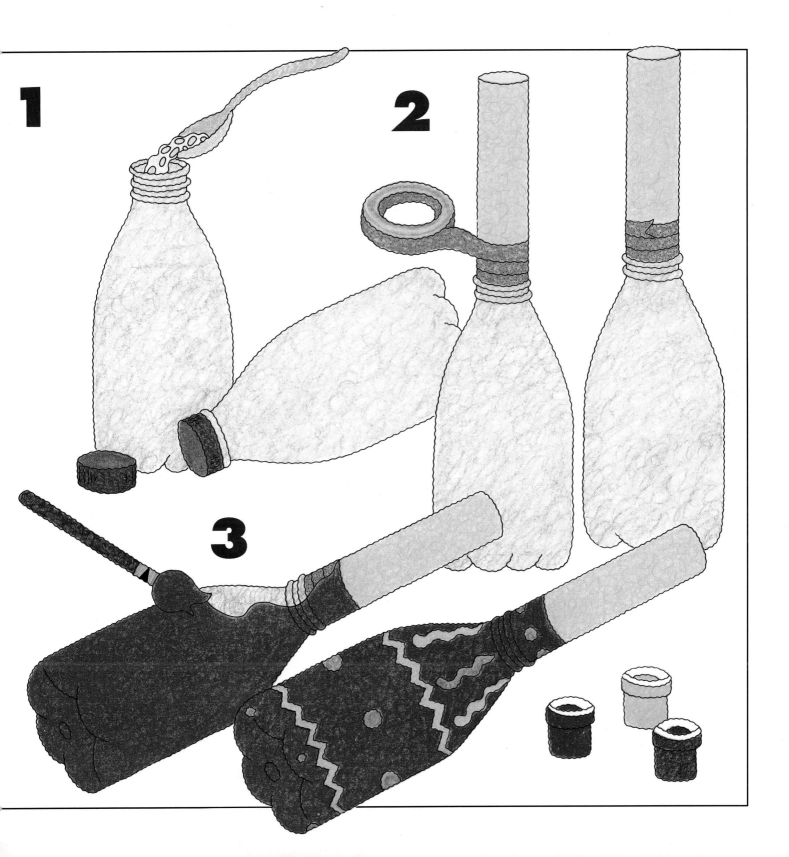

bracelets

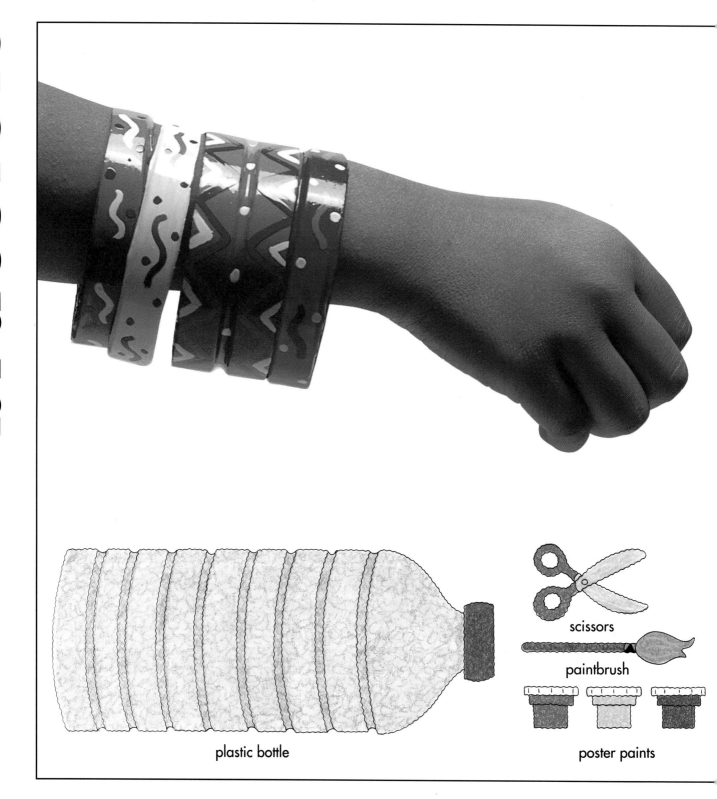

plastic bottle

scissors

paintbrush

poster paints

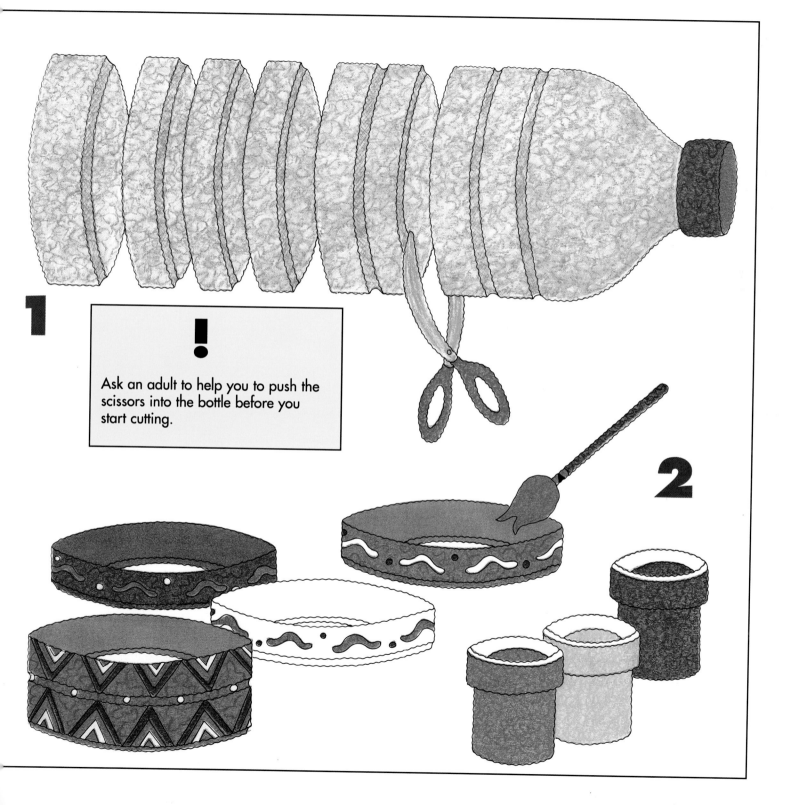

1

!

Ask an adult to help you to push the scissors into the bottle before you start cutting.

2

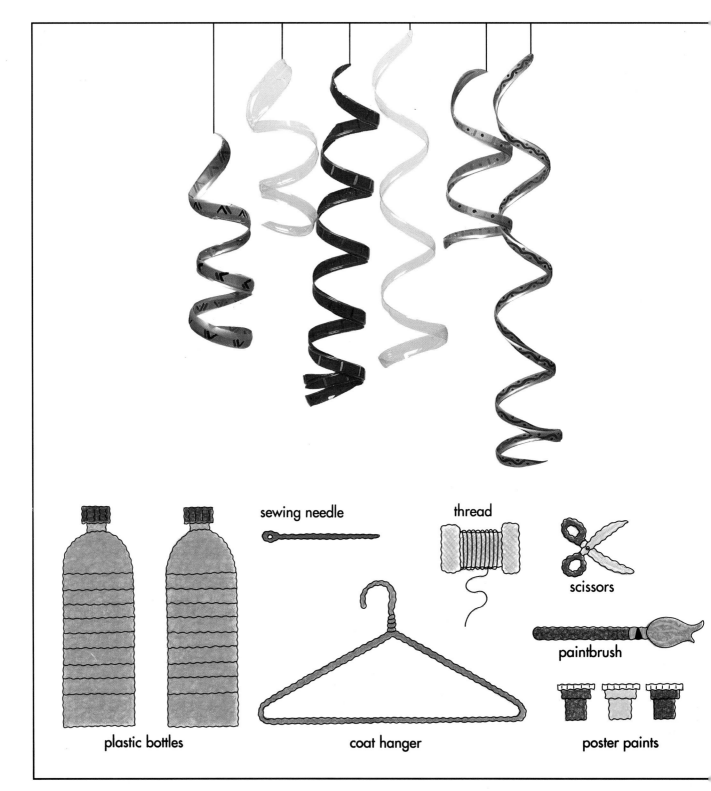

mobile

plastic bottles

sewing needle

thread

scissors

coat hanger

paintbrush

poster paints

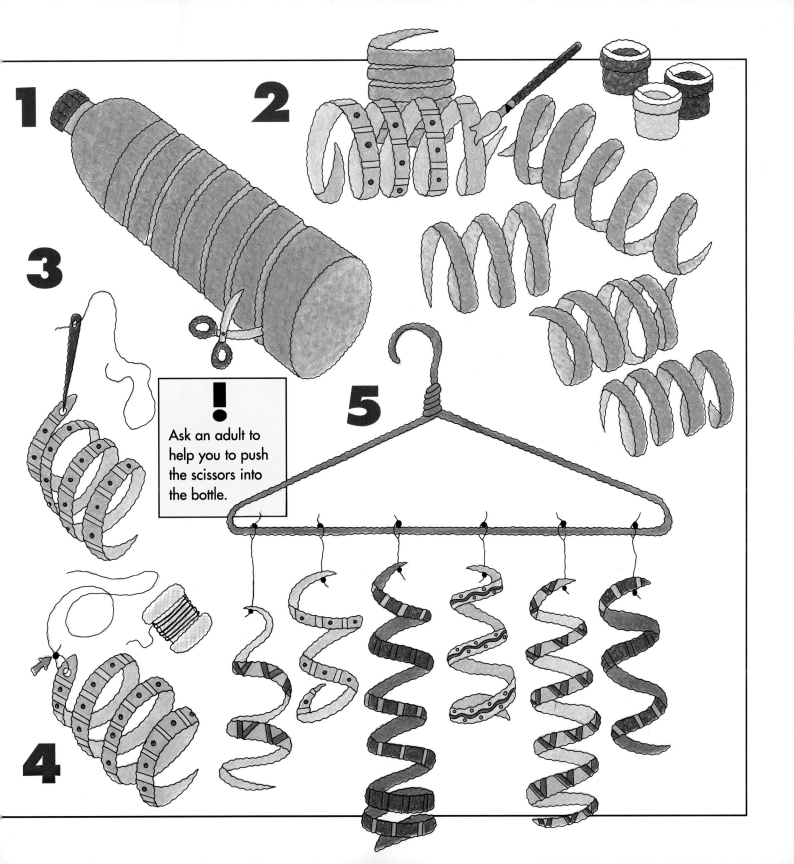

1

2

3

!
Ask an adult to
help you to push
the scissors into
the bottle.

4

5

submarine

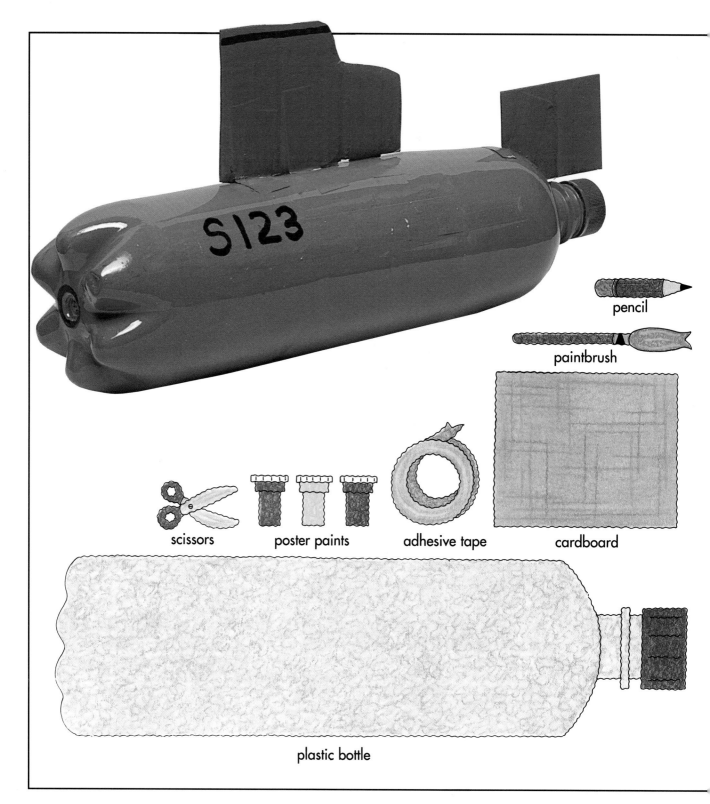

S123

pencil

paintbrush

scissors

poster paints

adhesive tape

cardboard

plastic bottle

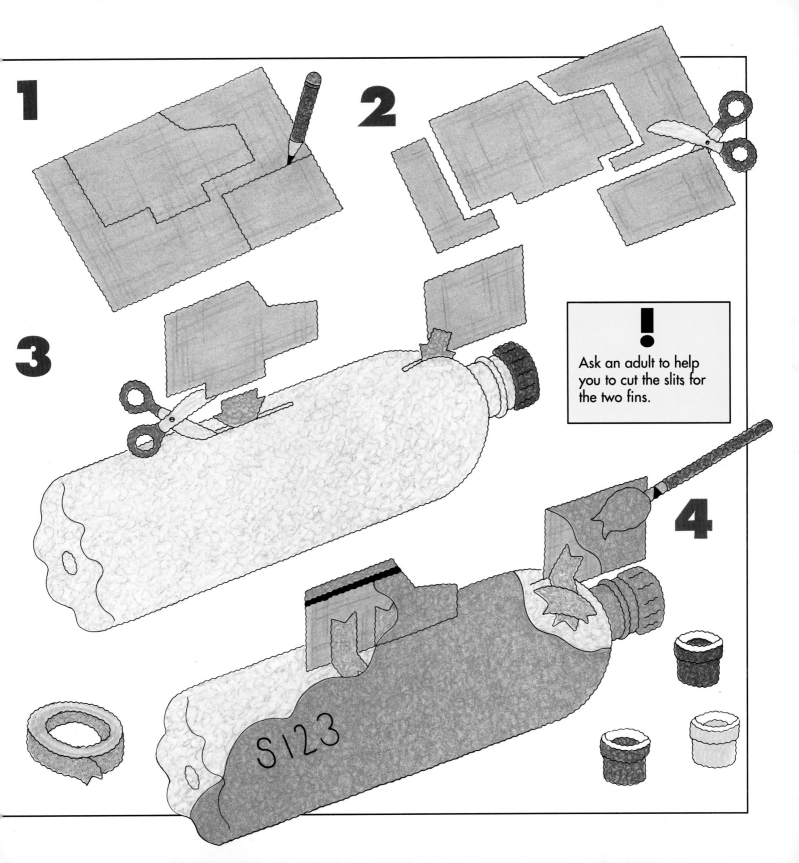

1

2

3

4

Ask an adult to help you to cut the slits for the two fins.

S123

windmill

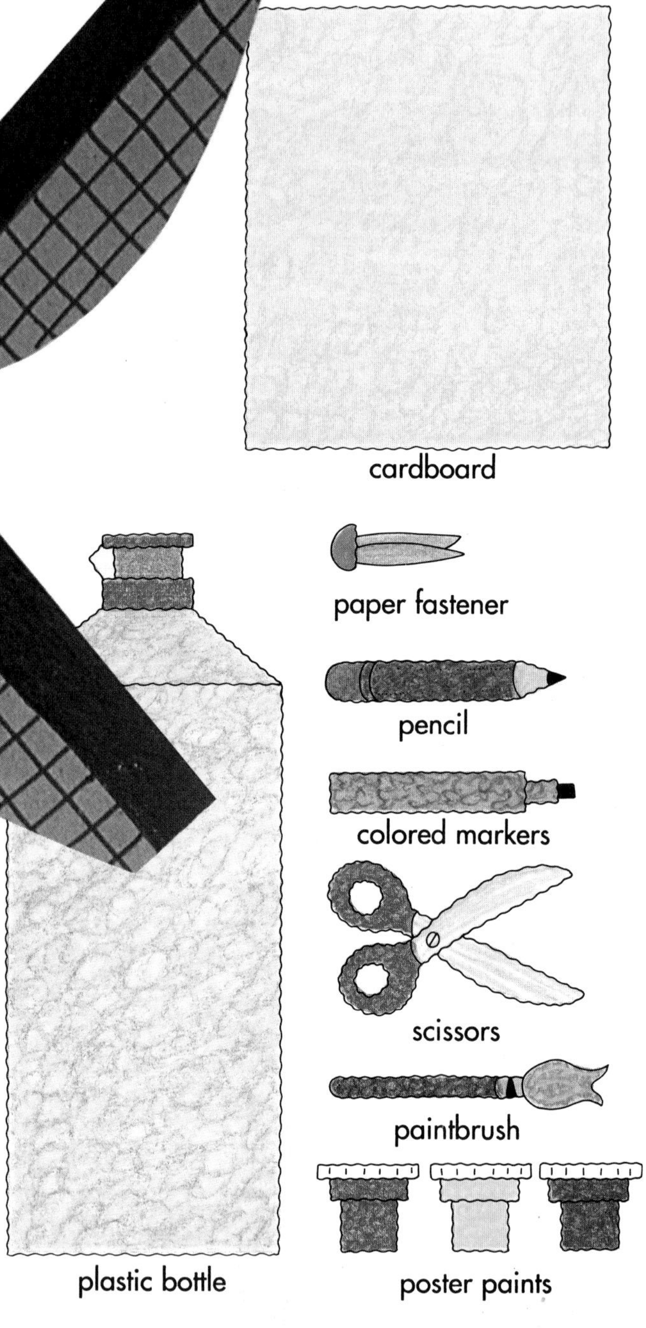

cardboard

paper fastener

pencil

colored markers

scissors

paintbrush

plastic bottle

poster paints

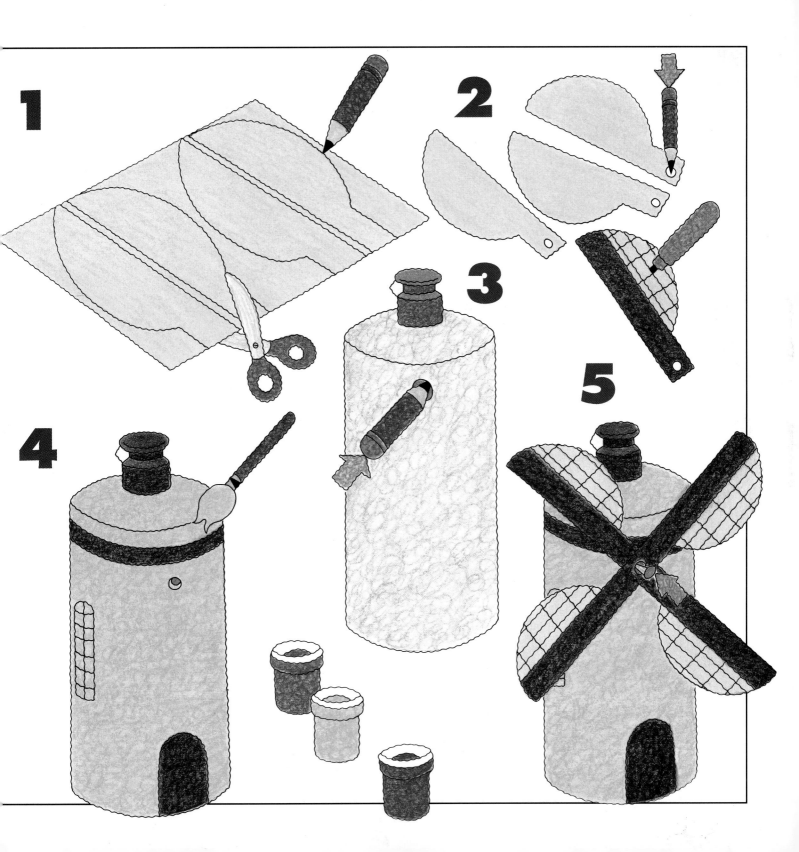

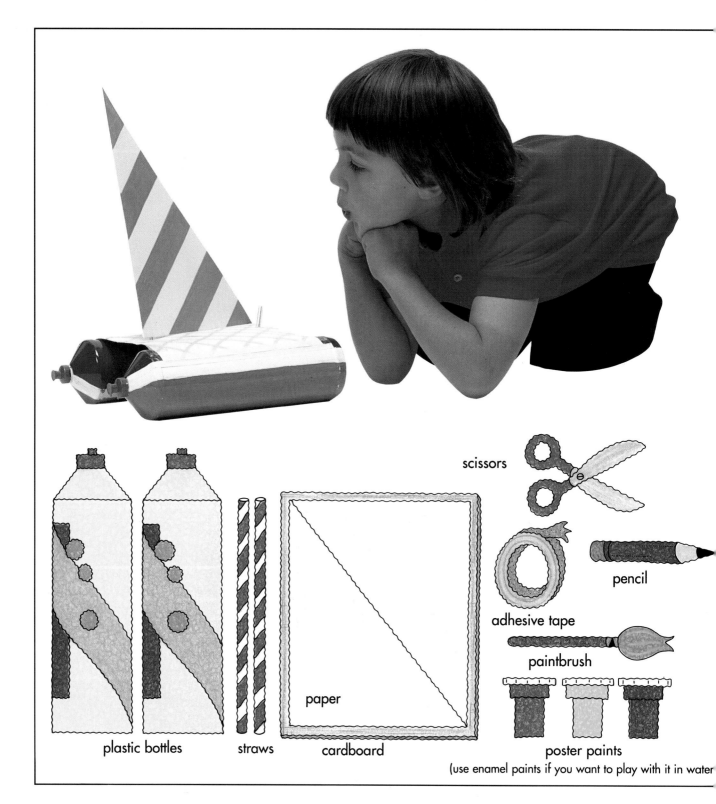

catamaran

scissors

pencil

adhesive tape

paintbrush

plastic bottles

straws

paper

cardboard

poster paints
(use enamel paints if you want to play with it in water

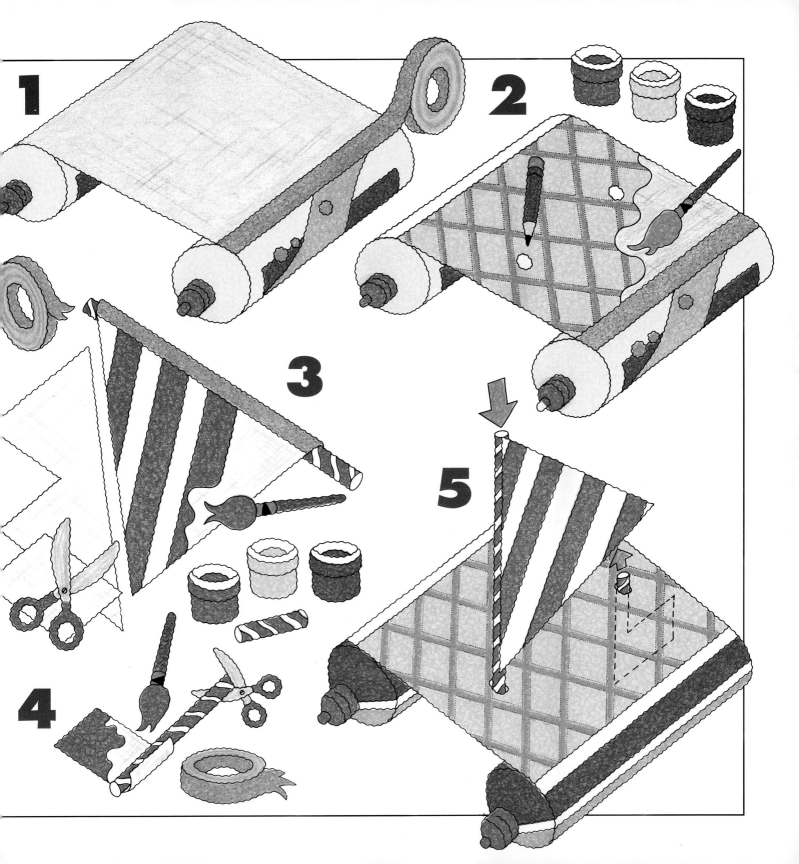

space shuttle

pencil

Velcro

paintbrush

glue

adhesive tape

plastic bottles

cardboard

scissors

poster paints

silver paint

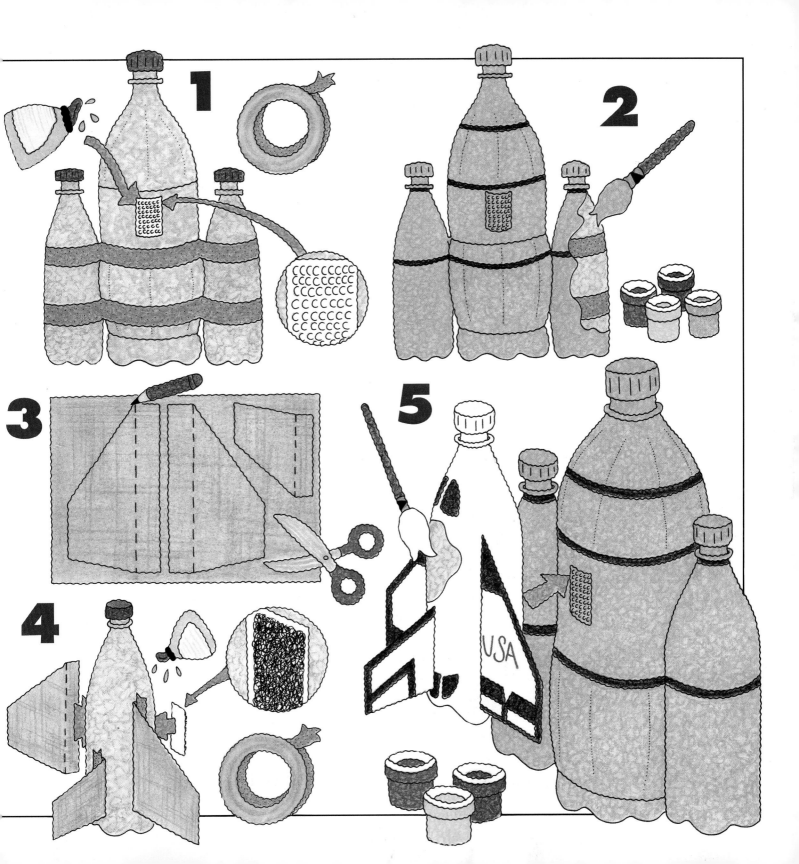

1

2

3

4

5

USA

racing car

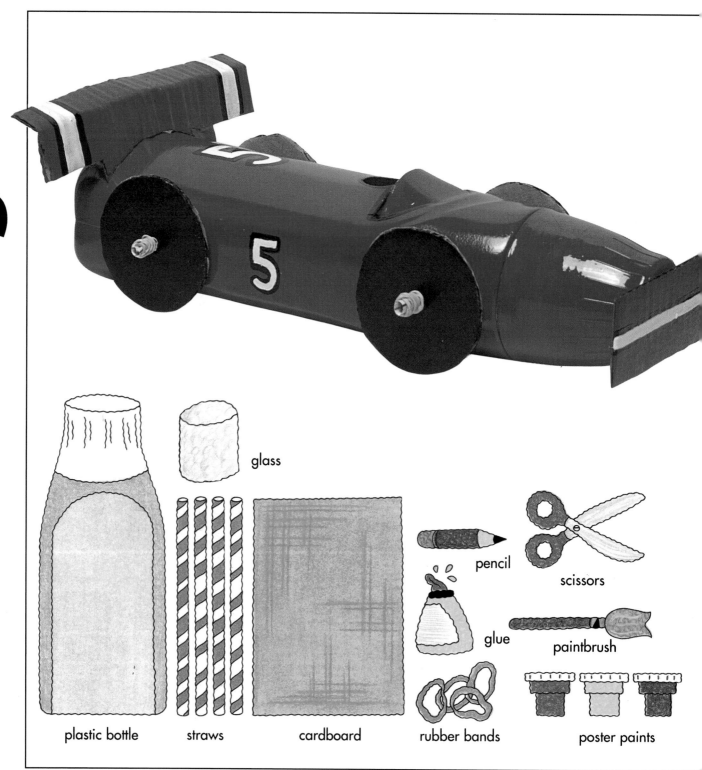

glass

plastic bottle

straws

cardboard

pencil

scissors

glue

paintbrush

rubber bands

poster paints

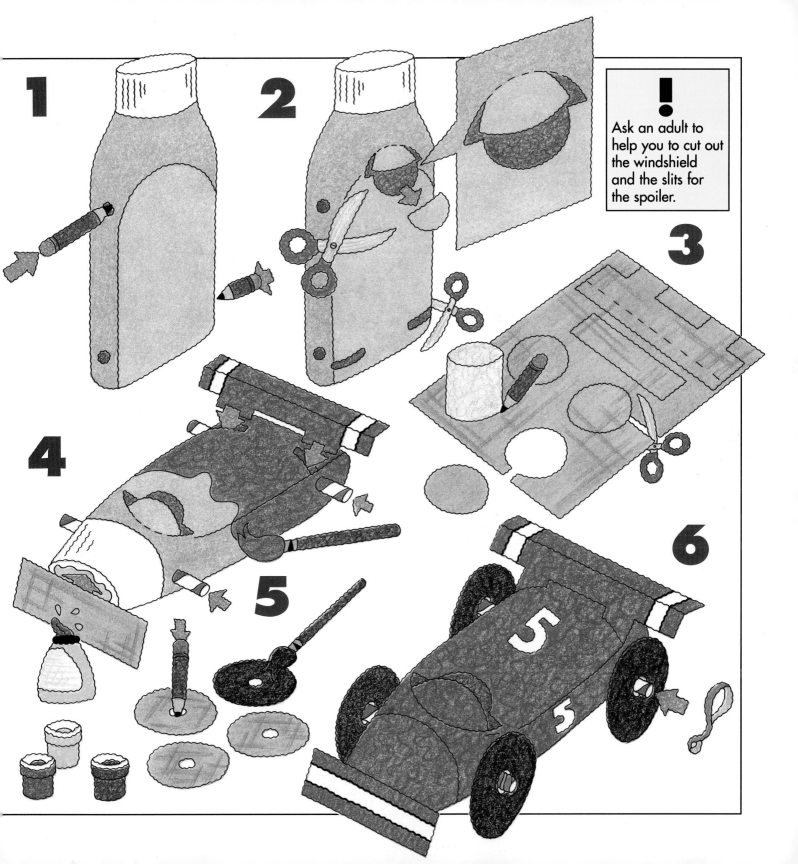

1

2

3

4

5

6

! Ask an adult to help you to cut out the windshield and the slits for the spoiler.

color chart

You can mix the three primary colors to make all the colors of the rainbow. Follow the chart below to mix the colors you want. The numbers on the cups show the proportions of each color you need to make the new color.

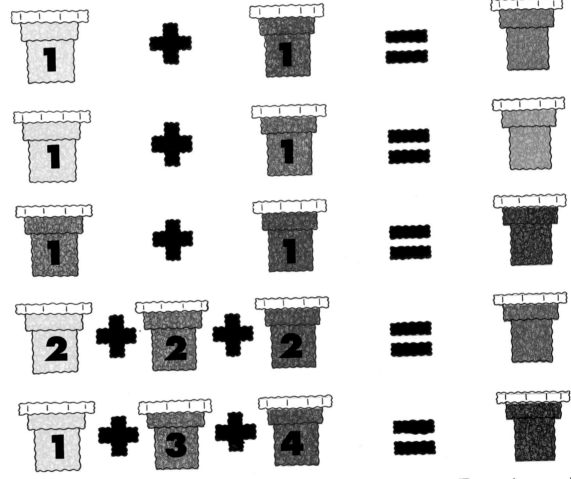

Different types of paint will give different results. Experiment by mixing different proportions of colors. Make sure you wash the brush before dipping it into each paint cup.